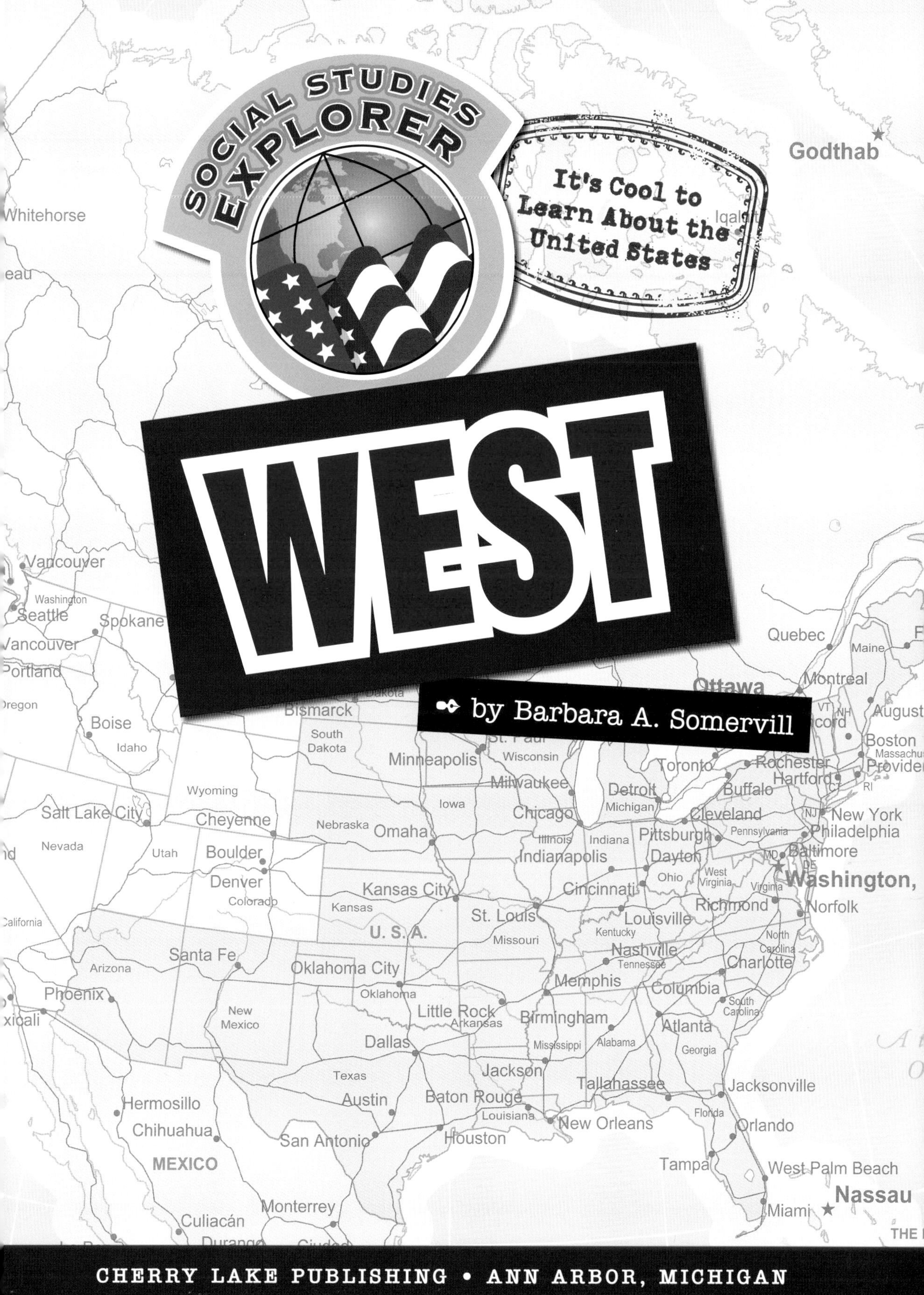
SOCIAL STUDIES EXPLORER
It's Cool to Learn About the United States
WEST
by Barbara A. Somervill
CHERRY LAKE PUBLISHING • ANN ARBOR, MICHIGAN

Published in the United States of America
by Cherry Lake Publishing
Ann Arbor, Michigan
www.cherrylakepublishing.com

Content Adviser: James Wolfinger, PhD, Associate Professor, History and Teacher Education, DePaul University, Chicago, Illinois

Book design: The Design Lab

Photo credits: Cover and page 1, ©iStockphoto.com/Davel5957, ©iStockphoto.com/cgering, ©iStockphoto.com/schutzphoto, ©iStockphoto.com/thunder; page 4, ©Johnathan Esper/Dreamstime.com; page 5, ©Pandkjar/Dreamstime.com; page 7, ©Zhou Minyun/Dreamstime.com; page 8, ©David R. Frazier Photolibrary, Inc./Alamy; page 9, ©jovannig/Shutterstock, Inc.; page 10, ©James Phelps Jr/ Dreamstime.com; page 11, ©Jay BeilerDreamstime.com; page 12, ©William Michael Norton/Dreamstime.com; page 13, ©Tony Campbell/Shutterstock, Inc.; page 14, ©John Warburton-Lee Photography/Alamy; page 15, ©NASA; pages 16, 24, 31, and 43, ©Media Bakery; page 17, ©Cecoffman/Dreamstime.com; page 18, ©Andre Nantel/Dreamstime.com; page 19, ©Gordon Swanson/Shutterstock, Inc.; page 20, ©North Wind Picture Archives/Alamy; page 22, ©ABN Images/Alamy; page 23, ©Donald Higgs/Alamy; page 25, ©iStockphoto.com/Peter Mah; page 26, ©Photos 12/Alamy; page 28, ©J. Norman Reid/Shutterstock, Inc.; page 29, ©Dennis MacDonald/Alamy; page 30, ©Andre Nantel/Dreamstime.com; page 32, ©Jerry Bernard/Dreamstime.com; page 33, ©Natalia Bratslavsky/Shutterstock, Inc.; page 35, ©Michal Maly/Dreamstime.com; page 36, ©Michael Smith/Dreamstime.com; page 37, ©Myrleen Pearson/Alamy; page 38, ©Ben Renard-wiart/Dreamstime.com; page 39, ©Jason Parks/Dreamstime.com; page 40, ©Alfredo Ragazzoni/Dreamstime.com; page 42, ©Teamcrucillo/Dreamstime.com

Library of Congress Cataloging-in-Publication Data
Somervill, Barbara A.
It's cool to learn about the United States: West/by Barbara A. Somervill.
p. cm.—(Social studies explorer)
Includes bibliographical references and index.
ISBN-13: 978-1-61080-182-9 (lib. bdg.)
ISBN-13: 978-1-61080-306-9 (pbk.)
1. West (U.S.)—Juvenile literature. I. Title. II. Title: West. III. Series.
F591.S6687 2011
978—dc22 2011003479

Cherry Lake Publishing would like to acknowledge the work of The Partnership for 21st Century Skills. Please visit *www.21stcenturyskills.org* for more information.

Printed in the United States of America
Corporate Graphics Inc.
July 2011
CLFA09

WEST

TABLE OF CONTENTS

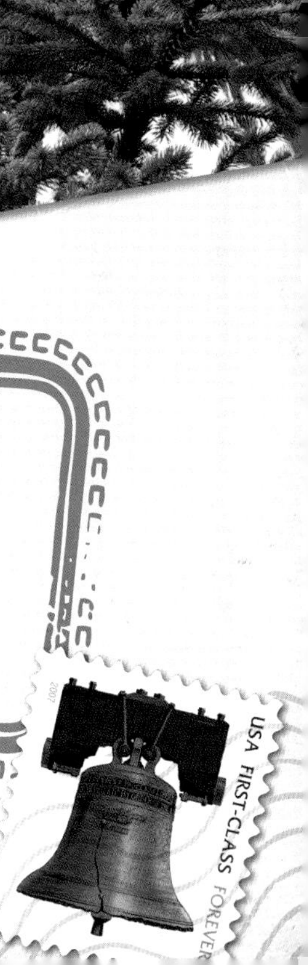

CHAPTER ONE

FROM DENALI TO DEATH VALLEY

Mountaineers camp in tents at the base of Denali in Alaska.

A party of mountaineers prepares to climb Alaska's Denali. Thousands of miles away, in the middle of the Pacific Ocean, tourists sun themselves on Waikiki Beach, Hawaii. More than 5,000 miles (8,000 kilometers) to the east, pink milkweed and yellow biscuit root grow on Colorado's San Juan Mountains. This wide range of natural beauty is the West at its best.

The West has varied geography, climate, animals, and plants. The region features tall mountains, deep valleys, and active volcanoes. It has hot deserts, tropical rain forests, and frozen tundra.

Eleven states make up this region. Alaska, California, Oregon, and Washington line the Pacific coastline. Nevada and Utah lie in the Great Basin. Colorado, Idaho, Montana, and Wyoming are Rocky Mountain states. Hawaii lies about 2,400 miles (3,800 km) off the West Coast of the United States.

Small huts sometimes stand near the beaches of the Hawaiian islands.

ACTIVITY

FIND THE STATE AND ITS CAPITAL

STOP
Don't write in this book!

Place a piece of tracing paper over the map of the West and trace the states' borders. Each star represents the location of a state capital. Look at the list to the right of the map and write the names of the capitals next to the stars in the correct states.

Juneau
Sacramento
Denver
Honolulu
Boise
Helena
Carson City
Salem
Salt Lake City
Olympia
Cheyenne

Answers: Alaska, Juneau; California, Sacramento; Colorado, Denver; Hawaii, Honolulu; Idaho, Boise; Montana, Helena; Nevada, Carson City; Oregon, Salem; Utah, Salt Lake City; Washington, Olympia; Wyoming, Cheyenne

Utah's Zion National Park is known for the cliffs that rise up as part of the Rockies.

MOUNTAINS, VOLCANOES, AND EARTHQUAKES

The Rocky Mountains dominate the West, rising through Montana, Idaho, Wyoming, Utah, and Colorado. The Rockies are clusters of mountain ranges that include Idaho's Cabinet and Salish Mountains, Montana's Bitterroot Range, and Colorado's Sangre de Cristo Mountains. Colorado has 54 peaks that are more than 14,000 feet (4,267 meters) high.

People in Pullman, Washington, clean up ash after the violent eruption of Mount St. Helens in May 1980.

The Pacific Coast Range runs along North America's West Coast. It includes the Sierra Nevadas, Columbia Mountains, and Cascades. Alaska's Kenai Mountains, Chugach Mountains, and Yukon Ranges are also Pacific Coast Range mountains. Many of these mountains are **dormant**, or not presently active, volcanoes.

The most powerful volcanic **eruption** in recent history was Mount St. Helens in Washington. After being dormant for more than 100 years, the volcano erupted on May 18, 1980. It was the deadliest volcanic event in

U.S. history. Mount Rainier in Washington and Lassen Peak in California are dormant volcanoes in the Pacific Coast Range. Volcanic mountains that rise from the Pacific Ocean floor make up the Hawaiian Islands. Hawaii's Mauna Loa and Kilauea are active volcanoes.

California and Alaska are prone to earthquake activity. The worst earthquake in recent history was the October 1989 Loma Prieta earthquake in California. It killed 63 people and caused about $7 billion in damage.

Denali, also known as Mount McKinley, is often called the coldest mountain in the world. Nighttime temperatures can sink below -40 degrees Fahrenheit (-40 degrees Celsius). Winds whip across the **summit**, which is the highest in North America at 20,320 feet (6,194 m).

THE GREAT BASIN AND MOJAVE DESERT

The Great Basin covers most of Nevada and Utah, and parts of Oregon and eastern California. It is "high" desert, a plateau where more than 800 different types of plants grow. Common plants include prickly pear cactus, sagebrush, and aspen. Mountain lions hunt in the high regions where pronghorn and bighorn sheep graze.

The Mojave Desert stretches from southeastern California into Nevada and Utah. There lies Death Valley, the lowest point in the United States at 282 feet (86 m)

Bighorn sheep travel in herds across the Mojave Desert.

Visitors to San Diego, California, can take advantage of the area's warm, sunny beaches.

below sea level. Temperatures in Death Valley regularly soar above 100°F (37.8°C). The landscape is filled with cacti, creosote bush, and yucca.

HOT, COLD, DRY, AND RAINY

The West features a variety of climates. Hawaii is tropical. It has warm days and nights, brief daily rainfall, and plenty of sunshine. San Diego in California is subtropical with warm summers and cool winters. Most of the West enjoys a moderate climate, with warm summers and cold winters. The mountain regions have cooler summers and cold winters.

Temperate rain forests along the Pacific Coast have unique **ecosystems**. There you will find redwoods, Douglas firs, western hemlocks, and western red cedars. In old-growth forests, fallen trees rot in the damp weather and provide a nursery for seedlings. Some of the trees in these forests are more than 1,000 years old. One of the world's oldest trees, named Methuselah, is a bristlecone pine that lives in the Inyo National Forest in California. Scientists believe that Methuselah is more than 4,700 years old!

Bristlecone pines grow slowly in cool, dry areas in the West.

Bald eagles can be seen in Wyoming and other western states.

ALL THINGS LIVING

Each western ecosystem balances animal and plant life. Major **predators**, such as wolves, mountain lions, and coyotes, hunt for deer, elk, and moose. In the coastal waters, orcas prey on seals and young whales. Smaller predators, such as foxes and badgers, feed on rodents, eggs, and birds. Owls swoop down in the night to capture ground squirrels and rats. Bald eagles feast on fish. Alaska has more bald eagles than any other state in the country.

The region's large plant-eaters include bighorn sheep, moose, pronghorn antelopes, and white-tailed deer. They munch their way through western shrubs, grasses, and wildflowers. Kangaroo rats, field mice, and rabbits feed on seeds, nuts, and berries. The West is home to the elf owl, America's smallest owl, and its largest bird, the California condor.

Every western state has many different plants and shrubs. Some, such as California poppies and blue columbines, sprinkle color on open fields and meadows. Others, such as prickly pear and barrel cactus, have sharp spines. Each state has its own unique plant life as well as many common varieties.

Syringa is the state flower of Idaho.

CHAPTER TWO

THE STORY OF THE WEST

The Bering Strait separates Alaska from Siberia.

Hunter-gatherers followed large game animals from Asia across the Bering Strait land bridge to North America. This happened sometime between 30,000 and 10,000 years ago. These early residents became the five major native peoples of Alaska: the Aleut, Athabascans, Tlingit,

Native clans in Alaska and elsewhere in the West used canoes or kayaks for fishing.

Inuit, and Yupik. These **clans** of Alaskans fished for salmon or hunted whale, walruses, bear, and moose. They lived in small villages and shared their food. Hunters braved the seas in small kayaks or in dugout canoes. Descendants of these early peoples still live in Alaska and belong to Native American societies.

HUMANS MOVE SOUTH

By 10,000 BCE, clans had moved south and east, eventually forming new native nations. In the Pacific Northwest, clans depended on salmon, seals, and whales for food and skins. Families lived in large houses with aunts, uncles, grandparents, and cousins.

Farther east, hunter-gatherer clans evolved into new tribes. We know them today as the Cheyenne, the Blackfoot, and the Shoshone. In present-day Utah, Colorado, and Nevada, tribes emerged as the Paiutes, the Utes, and the Arapaho. Native people lived off the land and took advantage of local fish and animals, such as clams, trout, and bison.

Hawaiians are the only native people who did not evolve from Asians who crossed the Bering land bridge. Between 300 and 500 AD, Polynesians from the Marquesas Islands arrived in the Hawaiian Islands. Around 1200, Tahitians conquered the Marquesans and settled on Hawaii.

EXPLORATION OF THE WEST

European exploration of the West began in the early 1500s when the Spanish conquered the Aztecs in present-day Mexico. Spanish explorers searched for gold and glory. Francisco Vásquez de Coronado and Juan Cabrillo claimed land for Spain's king. Between 1519 and 1542, Spain laid claim to the entire Southwest.

In 1741, the Russian czar sent Aleksei Chirikov and Vitus Bering to explore the seas east of Russia's Pacific coastline. They came upon Alaska but did not form a settlement there until 1784.

A statue of Juan Cabrillo stands in San Diego, California.

Lewis and Clark followed the Missouri River west from St. Louis, Missouri, into the Rockies.

In 1803, the United States bought an enormous amount of land in North America from the French, called the Louisiana Purchase. It doubled the size of the United States. President Thomas Jefferson sent Meriwether Lewis and William Clark to explore the land west of the Missouri River. Lewis and Clark's travels took them into the land of the Sioux, Shoshone, and Nez Perce. A Shoshone guide, Sacagawea, led them westward. Lewis and Clark met native peoples, and discovered rich lands and rivers abundant with fish.

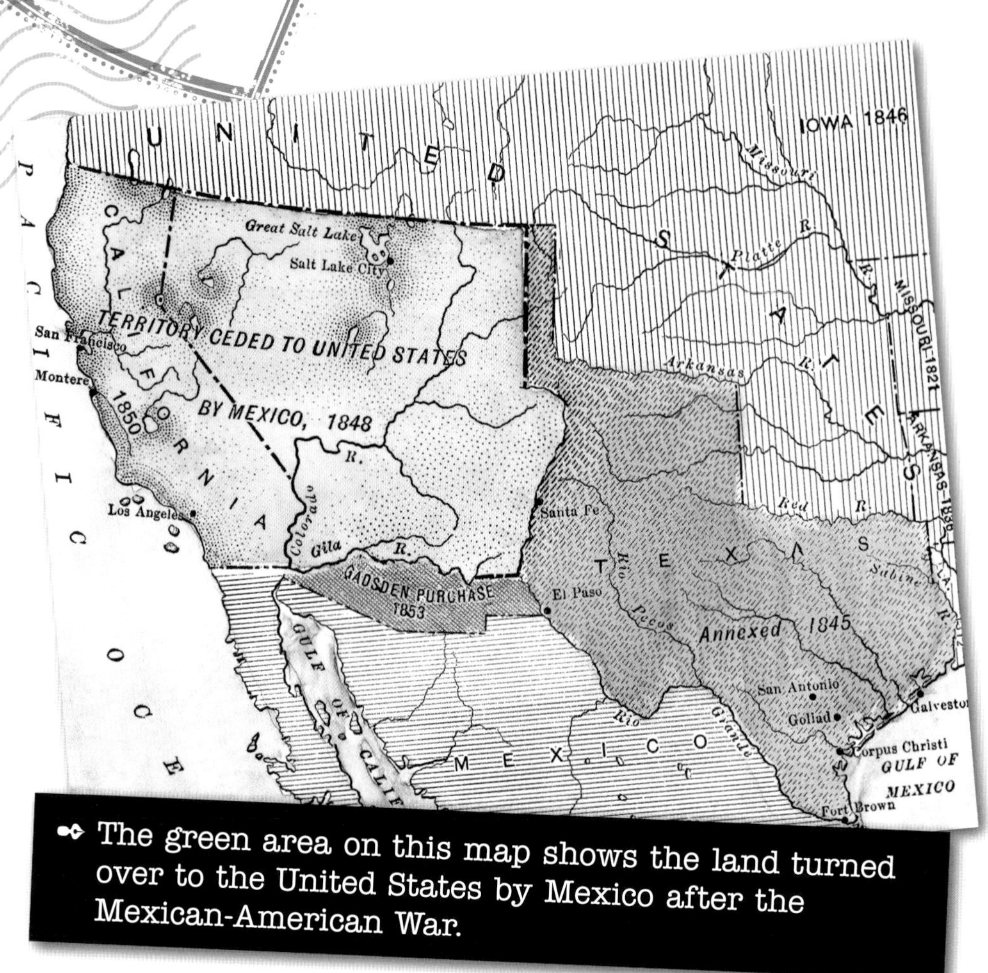

The green area on this map shows the land turned over to the United States by Mexico after the Mexican-American War.

Several years later, the United States fought against Great Britain in the War of 1812. After the war, the British and the United States both claimed Oregon. The land was in dispute until 1846, when the border was finally agreed to. Mexico controlled most of the region south of Oregon. From 1846 to 1848, the United States fought Mexico in the Mexican-American War. The United States won, and Mexico was forced to sell its northern territories to the United States. The Treaty of Guadalupe Hidalgo gave California, Nevada, Utah, Arizona, New Mexico, Texas, and parts of Wyoming and Colorado to the United States.

States in the West officially achieved statehood on the following dates:

STATE	DATE OF STATEHOOD	STATE NUMBER
California	September 9, 1850	31st
Oregon	February 14, 1859	33rd
Nevada	October 31, 1864	36th
Colorado	August 1, 1876	38th
Montana	November 8, 1889	41st
Washington	November 11, 1889	42nd
Idaho	July 3, 1890	43rd
Wyoming	July 10, 1890	44th
Utah	January 4, 1896	45th
Alaska	January 3, 1959	49th
Hawaii	August 21, 1959	50th

MANIFEST DESTINY

Few settlers had moved to the West before James Marshall discovered gold at Sutter's Mill, California, in 1848. More than 300,000 people flocked to the West during the Gold Rush, as miners sought their fortunes in California.

Trails to the West opened up from the area of the Mississippi River. The most-used trails were the Mormon Trail and the Oregon Trail. Farmers, ranchers, miners, and their families headed westward in long wagon trains. It took pioneers 4 to 6 months to reach their

The mill at which James Marshall found gold was rebuilt at the Marshall Gold Discovery State Historic Park.

You can visit the Blackfeet Indian Reservation in Montana.

destinations. With the growth of these new areas, many western states were added to the United States. The western expansion of the United States was considered by many Americans to be the country's Manifest Destiny. This was the name given to the belief that it was the fate of the United States to expand across North America.

As settlers filled the West, problems arose with Native American tribes. The U.S. government signed

treaties that moved the native peoples onto land with few game animals and poor soil. Native Americans starved and fought back in frequent armed conflicts with government soldiers.

The development of the railroad during the 1860s helped make travel to the west faster and more efficient. By 1885, four transcontinental lines connected the East and the West. Travel time was reduced from months to days.

In 1867, U.S. secretary of state William Seward arranged a deal with Russia to buy Alaska. The price was $7.2 million, or about 2.5¢ per acre (0.40 hectare). People called the purchase "Seward's Folly" and "Seward's Icebox." Those critics had no idea that Alaska had gold, silver, oil, fish, and timber worth a fortune.

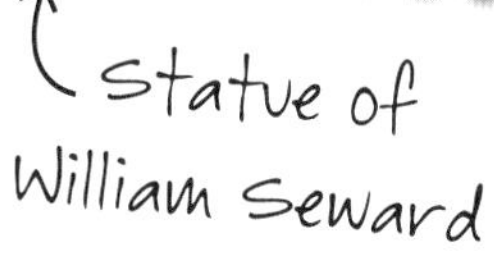

Statue of William Seward

The Ford Model T helped make travel easier in the early 20th century.

INTO THE 20TH CENTURY

New technologies brought major changes to the West in the 20th century. A network of railroads connected the West's larger cities. Cars and trucks made it easier for people to travel and for businesses to deliver products and services. Tractors replaced horse-drawn plows, making farming quicker and more productive. Telephones made communication faster and more reliable. Electricity supplied the power for lights and for an ever-growing number of machines in homes and factories.

Europe was torn by World War I from 1914 to 1918. To help the war effort, West Coast workers built ships and

The USS *Tennessee* and USS *Virginia* burn after the Japanese attack on Pearl Harbor on December 7, 1941.

airplanes, processed salmon and tuna, and cut timber. Farmers grew wheat, vegetables, and fruits. Ranchers provided beef, lamb, and pork. When the war ended, the West prospered. During the financial woes of the Great Depression in the 1930s, many Americans headed west in a new "gold rush"—the rush to find work.

On December 7, 1941, Japan attacked the American naval fleet at Pearl Harbor, Hawaii, killing and wounding thousands and destroying many ships and buildings. The United States was once again at war. West Coast men joined the military. Women began working in factories, building ships, and processing food.

MATCH THE WESTERNERS

Match the famous people in this list with their accomplishments.

NAME	ACCOMPLISHMENT
1. Sacagawea	a. Discovered gold in California
2. Brigham Young	b. Claimed Colorado for Spain
3. James Marshall	c. Arranged purchase of Alaska
4. Meriwether Lewis	d. Leader of an expedition across the West
5. William Seward	e. Shoshone guide
6. Francisco Vásquez de Coronado	f. Mormon leader

Answers: 1-e; 2-f; 3-a; 4-d; 5-c; 6-b

CHAPTER THREE

GOVERNMENT AND ECONOMY

They Wyoming state capitol is in Cheyenne, Wyoming.

State **constitutions** set up three branches of government: executive, legislative, and judicial. These bodies pass and enforce laws that apply to the people of each western state. Although each state in the West has its own laws, citizens must also follow federal, or national, laws.

THE EXECUTIVE BRANCH

The executive branch of state governments consists of the governor and departments or bureaus that oversee the workings of the state. The governor and advisers deal with the economy, education, and the environment. The governor's office is also responsible for public health and safety, transportation, agriculture, and the National Guard.

Most governors serve 4-year terms. Some states limit the number of terms for a governor to two terms, or 8 years in office. Governors appoint most department heads, but several states choose to elect people to key positions.

The governor of Oregon works out of this office in Salem, Oregon.

Colorado's State Senate meets in the senate chambers to discuss and vote on bills.

THE LEGISLATIVE BRANCH

The legislative branch makes a state's laws. The state legislature has a senate and either an assembly or a house of representatives. All laws passed in a state begin as a bill in either the Senate or the House of Representatives. The bill must pass by a majority in each house. The bill is then sent to the governor, who signs it into law or **vetoes** the bill.

Legislatures usually meet every year. In 1990, California and Colorado passed laws to limit the number of terms senators and representatives could serve. Since that time, several other states in the West have set term limits on lawmakers. However, those laws were overturned in Idaho, Oregon, Utah, Washington, and Wyoming.

JUDICIAL BRANCH

The judicial branch of a state government includes the judges, courts, and prison system. In trial courts, a judge and jury hear evidence about a case. The case may be criminal, such as robbery, or may be civil, such as a lawsuit over a contract.

Appellate courts hear complaints about trials that have already been held. A state's supreme court is the last appeal a person can make. It is also the place where laws are reviewed to determine if they follow the state's constitution.

The Nevada state supreme court used to meet in this room in the old state capitol building in Carson, Nevada.

Fire departments are one of many public services controlled by local governments.

LOCAL GOVERNMENTS

Local governments may be on the county, city, or town level. All states in the West have counties, except for Alaska, which is divided into 27 boroughs. Most are led by a commissioner and a county council who deal with services such as libraries, fire departments, or hospitals. An executive, usually a mayor, and a city council run city governments.

AGRICULTURE AND INDUSTRY

The West is a main center of agricultural production in the United States. It produces fruits, vegetables, grains, and cattle and other livestock. The heart of the United

States' fishing industry lies in this region. Industry is extensive in the West. It leads the country in the areas of technology, aerospace, entertainment, and tourism.

Western farmers are leaders in growing fruits and vegetables. Washington is the largest U.S. producer of apples, cherries, and pears. Two-thirds of all U.S. potatoes come from Idaho. Hawaiian farmers grow pineapples and sugarcane. Farmers in California grow more than 200 different crops, including salad vegetables, plums, and apricots. They also grow almonds, walnuts, avocados, and garlic.

Cattle graze on a ranch in Montana.

CATTLE PRODUCTION IN THE WEST

For several states in the West, raising cattle is an important agricultural industry. Read the chart below and answer the questions that follow.

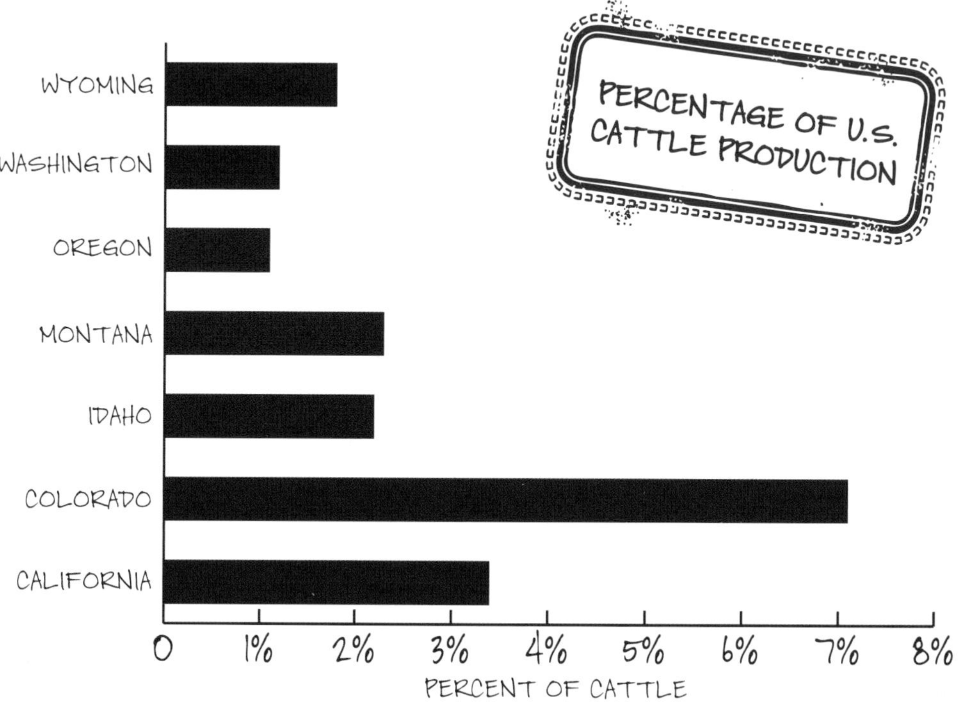

1. Which state produces the most cattle?
2. Which three states each account for less than 2 percent of U.S. cattle production?

Answers: 1-Colorado; 2-Oregon, Washington, and Wyoming

Montana, Nevada, Wyoming, Utah, and Idaho are major grain producers. Farmers in Idaho, Utah, and Montana grow wheat. Farmers in Nevada and Wyoming grow hay, barley, and corn. Colorado and California lead the region in raising cattle, although several other states produce beef cattle. Dairy farmers in Idaho, Alaska, Washington, and California raise dairy cattle for milk, butter, and cheese. California dairies produce about 20 percent of all U.S. dairy foods.

The West is a national leader in computer technology. California's Silicon Valley and Seattle, Washington, are home to well-known high-tech firms such as Apple, Hewlett-Packard, Intel, Cisco, Microsoft, and Adobe. Facebook, Twitter, eBay, and Google have headquarters in California's San Francisco Bay Area.

The West is also a center for tourism. Hawaii's beaches, California's cities, and Alaska's wilderness attract millions of tourists every year.

CHAPTER FOUR

PEOPLE OF THE WEST

San Francisco is one of California's most populated cities.

In the last 10 years, the population of the West has increased by 13.8 percent to 71,945,553 people. California is the largest state in the region and the nation, with 37,253,956 residents. Wyoming has the smallest population in the region and the country with 563,626 people.

The majority of people in the West are Caucasian. California has the largest percentage of Hispanic or Latino people. They make up 37 percent of its population. Nevada has 26.5 percent Hispanic residents. African Americans make up about 5 percent of the West's population. Nevada has the largest percentage of African Americans, at 8.3 percent.

Hawaii has the largest population of people with Asian backgrounds—38.8 percent—followed by California with 12.7 percent. California's Native American population, although the most in total numbers, represents a small percentage of the state's total population. Fifteen percent of Alaska's population is of native heritage.

The children in this California classroom come from many different ethnic backgrounds.

OUTDOOR LIVING

Outdoor living is definitely part of the western lifestyle. Hunting, fishing, surfing, and hiking feed residents' passion for their forests, mountains, and beaches.

There is an abundance of national parks and preserves in the West. Idaho, Montana, and Wyoming share Yellowstone National Park. It is the country's oldest national park, founded in 1872. The largest park is Alaska's Wrangell-St. Elias. Others include Glacier in Montana, Bryce Canyon in Utah, and Colorado's Rocky Mountain National Park.

Old Faithful geyser is one of the most famous attractions at Yellowstone National Park.

Dogsled team members must be trained from the time they are puppies.

Surfing is a popular sport in Hawaiian waters. Ski resorts in the Rockies attract skiers and snowboarders. Perhaps the most demanding sporting event in the West is Alaska's Iditarod. For about 2 weeks, mushers and their dogsled teams race from Anchorage to Nome across harsh Alaskan wilderness.

CELEBRATIONS AND FABULOUS FOOD

The origins of traditional arts and music of the West are traced to cowboys and Native Americans. Hoedowns blend square dancing, quick fiddling, and fast stepping. The square dance is the state dance of California, Colorado, Oregon, Utah, and Washington. Hawaiians

Mariachi bands are part of many Cinco de Mayo celebrations.

celebrate special days with luaus and the hula. Hula dancers tell stories with their hands.

Cinco de Mayo, the 5th of May, is a national holiday in Mexico. It is also enthusiastically celebrated in California, Nevada, and Colorado. Festivals feature Mexican foods, folk dancing, and piñatas.

The West is known for cookouts, fresh fruits and vegetables, tasty beef, and fresh fish. During peak seasons, roadside stands sell sweet cherries, crisp apples, and juicy apricots. Pacific Coast dwellers feast on Dungeness crabs, abalone, king crabs, and salmon. Hawaiians delight in mahimahi, grilled fresh pineapple, and traditional poi. Alaskans dine on bear steaks and moose burgers.

Try this quick and easy recipe for a delicious chili you will always come back to. Make sure you get an adult to help you cook the meal.

Chuckwagon Chili

INGREDIENTS

- 1 pound ground beef
- 1 small onion, chopped
- 1 green pepper, chopped with seeds removed
- 1 14-ounce can red kidney beans, drained and rinsed
- 1 14-ounce can navy beans, drained and rinsed
- 1 14-ounce can diced tomatoes
- 1 teaspoon chili powder
- 1 teaspoon salt
- ½ teaspoon black pepper

INSTRUCTIONS

1. In a Dutch oven with a lid, brown the beef, onion, and green pepper over medium heat. Brown for about 10 minutes, stirring until the meat is cooked.
2. Add all the other ingredients. Stir and cover. Simmer on low for 20 minutes. Serve with corn bread.

Serves 4; cooking time 30 minutes

Some people top their bowls of chili with cheese and fresh onion.

Cowboys had to stop and camp along the trail as they drove cattle across the West.

In the past, western meals were shared around a campfire. When the meal ended, it was time for poetry, music, and storytelling. Many poems and songs were about being on the range and away from home. The stories were often tall tales of mountain men and cowboy heroes. Today, stories are still told around campfires and the Old West spirit lives on.

FAST FACTS

Population (2009): 71,945,553

Total area of region: 1,531,454 square miles (3,966,448 sq km)

Highest point: 20,320 ft (6,194 m) Denali, Alaska

Lowest point: 282 ft (86 m) below sea level, Death Valley, California

Highest recorded temperature: 134°F (56.7°C) in Death Valley, California, on July 10, 1913

Lowest recorded temperature: -80°F (-62.2°C) in Prospect Creek Camp, northern Alaska, on January 23, 1971

Largest cities (2009): Los Angeles, California (3,831,868); San Diego, California (1,306,301); San Jose, California (964,695); San Francisco, California (815,358); Seattle, Washington, (617,334)

Professional Sports Teams:

Major League Baseball: Colorado Rockies, Los Angeles Angels, Los Angeles Dodgers, Oakland Athletics, San Diego Padres, San Francisco Giants, and Seattle Mariners

Major League Soccer: Chivas USA, Colorado Rapids, Los Angeles Galaxy, Portland Timbers, Real Salt Lake, San Jose Earthquakes, and Seattle Sounders

National Basketball Association: Denver Nuggets, Golden State Warriors, Los Angeles Clippers, Los Angeles Lakers, Portland Trail Blazers, Sacramento Kings, and Utah Jazz

National Football League: Denver Broncos, Oakland Raiders, San Diego Chargers, San Francisco 49ers, and Seattle Seahawks

National Hockey League: Anaheim Ducks, Colorado Avalanche, Los Angeles Kings, and San Jose Sharks

appellate (uh-PEL-it) having the power to listen to and decide on court appeals

clans (KLANZ) large groups of families descended from a common ancestor

constitutions (kahn-sti-TOO-shuhnz) documents that establish governments

dormant (DOR-muhnt) asleep or inactive

ecosystems (EE-koh-sis-tuhmz) communities of organisms and their environment

eruption (i-RUHP-shuhn) the ejection of molten rock, steam, or ash from a volcano

predators (PRED-uh-turz) animals that hunt other animals for food

summit (SUHM-it) the highest point

temperate (TEM-pur-it) not subject to long periods of extreme hot or cold weather

treaties (TREE-teez) agreements between two governments or groups over land, peace, or commerce

vetoes (VEE-tohz) stops a bill from becoming law

BOOKS

Friedman, Mel. *The Oregon Trail.* New York: Children's Press, 2010.

Harrison, Peter. *The Amazing World of the Wild West: Discover the Trailblazing History of Cowboys, Outlaws, and Native Americans*. London: Southwater, 2010.

Kent, Deborah. *Hawai'i.* New York: Children's Press, 2008.

McEvoy, Anne. *The American West.* New York: Chelsea House, 2009.

WEB SITES

Geographic Perspectives: Pacific Northwest
www.nbii.gov/portal/server.pt/community/pacific_northwest/241
The Pacific Northwest is made up of Washington, Idaho, and Oregon. Learn about its plants, animals, and ecosystems.

PBS: New Perspectives on the West
www.pbs.org/weta/thewest/program/
Check out this site about the West, its people, places, and events.

Trails West
www.over-land.com/trwestmid.html
Learn about the historic trails to the West and the people who traveled them.

INDEX

ABOUT THE AUTHOR
Barbara Somervill has lived in California and traveled across much of the West. She has been in every western state except Alaska, and that is definitely on the list for a future vacation. "Writing a book about the West," she says, "is like going on a marvelous journey. You get to visit the past, fabulous national parks, and interesting cities."